Brighter Grammar

An English Grammar with Exercises

BOOK TWO
New Edition

Phebean Ogundipe
C. E. Eckersley
Margaret Macaulay

Pearson Education Limited
Edinburgh Gate, Harlow,
Essex CM20 2JE, England
and Associated Companies throughout the world.

This edition first published 1983
20 19 18 17 16 15 14 13 12
IMP 42 4140 39 38 37
Set in 10/12 Helvetica

Printed in Malaysia, VP

ISBN 978-0-582-60972-3

Preface

This is a new edition of *Brighter Grammar.* The continued popularity of this book, over the years, has shown that the necessity of grammar in the learning of a language is appreciated, not only by curriculum planners and teachers of English, but also by the students. School students like to have a handy revision book to reinforce lessons. Private students need a clear yet concise course to bring their competence in English to the level required, either to facilitate their further studies in professional fields, or for increased efficiency at their work places.

The success of *Brighter Grammar* has been due firstly to the fact that the subject is made completely understandable to even the least linguistically-minded student, by presenting it as simply and as clearly as possible. In the course only the essentials of grammar have been chosen, and these have been explained with the minimum of technical terms. Only those terms are taught which are necessary to understand the structure of the language and to aid the student's progress in all essential aspects, including composition.

Secondly, to show that the learning of grammar can be as enjoyable as that of any subject in the curriculum, the books have been made as lively and amusing as possible. Stories have been used as material for exercises and for 'report' work in the composition lessons. The sentences in the exercises have been made as 'real' as possible, and the four books brightened by lively drawings.

In addition, special attention has been paid to the exercises, which are graded. and nothing is asked of the student that he cannot answer from the lesson on which the exercise is based. Also, wherever necessary, the lessons in Book 2, Book 3 and Book 4 are preceded by a revision of the work covered in the earlier book or books.

This new edition will make *Brighter Grammar* even more useful than before. The course has been completely revised, and the improvements fall into three major categories:

1 Greater relevance to the African scene by the modification or even removal of culturally distant examples and stories, replacing them with usages, examples and stories more familiar to the African student.

2 Up-dating and modernising of the linguistic material to Take into account the changes of idiom and usage which have made obsolete, or at least antiquated, certain items in the original edition. This up-dating is even more important to the African student than the editing or removal of references to a foreign culture. Any alert African student of English is aware that he is likely to come across references to a culture different from his own, and is therefore prepared to recognise and make efforts to understand them. However if periodic up-dating is not done, the student may find himself carefully learning some idiom or usage which, when used, will sound odd or outlandish to a contemporary native English speaker.

3 Occasional expansion or analysis of some grammatical points, so as to supply information which the original edition apparently assumed to be already known to the student. This filling in of gaps will be helpful to every student, especially those using the books on their own outside a classroom situation.

The authors therefore hope that *Brighter Grammar,* in this new and improved form, will continue to aid students, and give some relief to overburdened teachers, for many years to come.

Phebean Ogundipe
Lagos, Nigeria

Contents

1 Parts of Speech

Revision (from Book 1). There are eight parts of speech. They are **Nouns** (names of anything), **Pronouns** (words standing instead of nouns), **Adjectives** (words telling more about nouns), **Verbs** (words expressing an action or state of being), **Adverbs** (words telling more about verbs), **Conjunctions** (joining words), **Prepositions** (words used with nouns or pronouns to make phrases), **Interjections** (words used to express a sudden feeling).

If you are asked, 'What part of speech is *watch*?' or 'What part of speech is *iron*?" the right answer is, 'I don't know; but if you will put the word into a sentence, then I can give you the answer.'

Now why is this? It's because you tell what part of speech a word is by the work it is doing. And you can't always tell what work a word does until you see it at work in a sentence.
Take *watch*, for example, in the sentence,

My father gave me a new *watch* for my birthday.

You'll all agree that here *watch* is the name of something, and so it is a noun.
Now look at this sentence,

I am going to *watch* a football match.

Here, of course, *watch* is used to express an action, it tells what I am going to do. So in this sentence *watch* is a verb.
What about this sentence?

No burglars dare come to our house while we have a *watch* dog like Rex.

What sort of a dog? – a *watch* dog. As you know, words that tell 'what sort' are adjectives; so here, *watch* is an adjective describing the noun 'dog'.

Or take the word *dance* in these three sentences:

1 The dance went on till 3 a.m.

2 Can you dance?

3 At my cousin's request, the band played some dance music.

In 1 it is the name of something – a NOUN.

In 2 it expresses an action – a VERB.

In 3 it tells what sort of music – an ADJECTIVE.

So remember:

> **You tell what part of speech a word is by the work it does.**

Exercises

A What part of speech are the words in italics?

1 Use a big *hammer* for those *nails*.
2 *Hammer* the *nails* in well.
3 *Nail* the picture to the wall.
4 I can *answer* that question.
5 Give me the *answer* to the question.
6 We are going to *stay* in Athens.
7 We are not making a long *stay* there; only a week.
8 We *drink* tea from tea-cups.
9 Will you come and have a *drink*?
10 My father likes to *smoke* a pipe.
11 The *smoke* is going up the chimney.

B Give the part of speech of the words in italics.

1 He went to the *bath*room to *bath*.
2 First clean the *bath*, then *bath* the baby and dry him with the *bath* towel.

3 John's mother is using an electric *iron* to *iron* John's shirts.
4 That *iron* gate is made of *iron* that came from Aladja.
5 These *plants* need *water*; you should *water* them every day in dry weather.
6 I am going to *plant* some *water*-lilies in my pond.
7 I want you to *colour* these pictures any *colour* you like.

C Use the following words in sentences (a) as nouns and (b) as verbs (2 sentences for each word).

1 walk	**2** work	**3** use	**4** box	**5** fly
6 sack	**7** wish	**8** wave	**9** rain.	

D Here is a short story called

Don't Read Only the Headlines, Timi – Part 1

Mr Odu was in the sitting-room reading the newspaper. Timi, who stood behind him, was surprised to see over his father's shoulder:

BANK DANCES TILL DAY-BREAK

'But, Papa,' said Timi, 'that's strange! How can a Bank dance? Does the newspaper editor think the readers are stupid?'

'No, Timi,' said his father with a smile. 'It's you who have made the mistake of reading just the headline and reaching the wrong conclusion from it. Let me read you the whole story, and then you will understand the headline correctly.'

Timi's father then read out the following story:

Two dances planned by the United National Bank in Iba will set a new fashion this year – they will, literally, be till day-break.

The Management will be holding their annual end-of-year dance at which long-service awards and retirement gifts are presented, and senior and junior staff have a chance to meet one another socially. The second dance, a week or two later, is an inaugural dance at which the Junior Workers will be launching their newly-formed Association of Junior Bank Workers.

Both dances would normally have been from 9 p.m. until about 2 a.m., but because of the dusk-to-dawn curfew imposed after the recent disturbances in the town, the organisers decided that, instead of cancelling the dances, they should hold them all night until the end of curfew at 6 a.m.

What parts of speech are *bank* and *dances* in the headline? What parts of speech did Timi think they were?

2 Nouns

Revision (Book 1, pages 1 to 24). A noun is the name of anything. Nouns that are the names given to all people or things or places of the same kind are called **Common Nouns**. The names of particular persons, places or things are called **Proper Nouns**. Proper nouns all begin with a capital letter.

Nouns have number; singular number for one, plural number for more than one.

The Possessive case of singular nouns is formed by putting *'s* after the noun that stands for the possessor.

The Possessive case of plural nouns is formed by putting an apostrophe after the noun if the plural ends in 's' or by putting *'s* after the noun if the plural does not end in 's'.

The possessive form is not generally used for things, only for people (and for most animals).

Abstract Nouns

There are one or two other kinds of nouns that you ought to know. Look at these sentences:

The car went at a speed of 90 miles an hour.
The teacher showed me great kindness.
Tommy has toothache.
He bore the pain with great courage.
Health is better than wealth.

The words *speed, kindness, toothache, pain, courage, health, wealth* are all nouns: each of them is the name of something. But they are not quite like the other nouns that you have met so far. They are not so much the name of things as the name of qualities or ideas. They don't exist in the material world; you can't physically touch them. We know they exist, and the person with a bad tooth can certainly feel the 'ache', but he can only touch the tooth itself, not the 'toothache'. Similarly, you can hear the truth (or a falsehood) yet you can't see 'truth' with your two eyes, or touch it with your hands. We can even say that we see the whiteness of a piece of chalk, or the blueness of the sky, yet we can't hold 'blueness' or 'whiteness' in our hands, whereas we can hold a piece of chalk and break it into two pieces.

Whiteness, speed, health, etc., are not material things; they are abstract things. And nouns like this are called **Abstract Nouns**.

Collective Nouns

There are some nouns that are the names, not of just one person or thing, but of a whole collection of people or things, considered as one.

For example, in the school's football team there are eleven players but we think of it as *a* team, that is as *one* thing.

Here's the school choir singing in this year's Schools' Choral Competition. You don't think of the singers in each of the choirs as individual pupils but as one school choir competing against another choir.

Nouns that stand for a number of things considered as one are called **Collective Nouns**. Collective nouns generally (but not always) take a singular verb, e.g.

The crowd *was* one of the largest I have ever seen.

A flock of sheep *is* coming down the hill.

The class *has* an English lesson every day.

Exercises

A Pick out the abstract nouns in the following:

1 The soldiers fought with great courage.
2 He has always had very good health.
3 The flight of the birds was very beautiful.
4 I did my work without any help.
5 That flower has a pretty colour.
6 He was filled with admiration for my skill in rowing the boat.
7 The explorer was suffering from hunger and thirst but was full of hope for success.
8 There is wisdom in the old man's advice.
9 I want you to get the measurements of this room. Write down its length, breadth and height.
10 We all admire beauty, not ugliness; strength not weakness; bravery not cowardice; kindness not cruelty; generosity not meanness.

B Pick out the collective nouns in the following:

1 The man was driving a herd of cattle.
2 That ship has a crew of a hundred men.
3 He has a whole library of books.
4 A swarm of bees flew out of the hive.
5 The audience listened in complete silence to the singer.
6 A battalion* of soldiers is being sent to Chad.
7 Our cat has a litter of six tiny kittens.

8 The fishermen saw a big shoal of fish.
9 The police were trying to control the mob.
10 Recruits are wanted for the army*, the navy and the air force.

*(There are several collective nouns for soldiers, which vary according to the numerical size of the unit involved.)

C Pick out the nouns in the following story and arrange them in columns under the headings:

Common	Proper	Abstract	Collective

Twentieth Century Adventurers

Tourism has today taken the place held by exploration of distant lands in earlier centuries. It satisfies the feelings which sent men like Livingstone, Barth and Mungo Park travelling round Africa in the nineteenth century. The first of these is restlessness, the inability to sit down tamely in known surroundings, carrying out familiar daily tasks. Most explorers, including Marco Polo who made journey after journey to the Far East, Vasco da Gama who sailed round the Cape of Good Hope, and Columbus who reached America across the Atlantic, have been men who had this urge to travel to far-away places.

Next is the curiosity to see foreign people and learn foreign customs, to find out the truth about incredible 'facts' gathered from travellers' tales, or to test some theory of geography such as whether the earth is round or flat, or in which range of hills a

certain river has its source. Then there is the love of physica[l ex]ertion, the wish to carry out a difficult feat, such as climbing Mount Everest, the love of danger and the excitement of facing the unknown.

Today's tourists try to satisfy the same feelings but in rather different ways. There are no longer any mysteries of geography to solve. But restlessness still makes them fly thousands of miles away to some foreign country, and curiosity, when they reach there, urges them to see the local landmarks, try the local food, buy local crafts, and study the customs of the local people. And some of them seek danger or excitement, watching packs of lions in Kenya or making daring underwater swims among the dangerous coral reefs of the Pacific.

3 Plurals of Nouns

Revision (Book 1, pages 6 to 13). Singular nouns generally make their plurals by adding 's'.

Some (ending in 'sh, ch, x, s,' or in 'o') add 'es'.
Some (ending in 'f' or 'fe') change to 'ves'.
Some (ending in 'y') change to 'ies'.
Some are irregular.

In Book 1 you were given the principal methods of forming the plural. Now here is some more information about some of the irregular nouns.

1 A few nouns have the same form for singular or plural. The most commonly used of these nouns are *sheep* and *deer*.
For example:

Singular There is a *sheep* in the field.
Plural There are some *sheep* in the field.
Singular I saw a *deer* in the forest.
Plural I saw two *deer* in the forest.

Sometimes *fish* has the same form in the singular as in the plural, e.g.

The woman still had a lot of unsold *fish* in her basket.

2 Some nouns have no plural, e.g.

information, advice, furniture, news, etc.

So we say,

I bought three pieces of *furniture* (not 'three furnitures').

He gave me two good bits of *advice* (not 'two advices').

The *news* is good (not 'the news are good').

News looks like a plural word, but it isn't.

Brother has two plurals, *brothers* and *brethren*; but *brothers* is the one in common use – *brethren* is reserved for formal or solemn address to members of a profession, association or religious group.

3 Some nouns have no singular, e.g.

scissors, trousers, clothes, riches, people.

These *scissors* are not sharp (or This *pair of scissors* is not sharp).

Aliu's *trousers* were torn when he was climbing the tree.

Her *clothes* are always very smart.

Riches do not always bring happiness.

The *people* in this room have all come to see you.

4 There are some nouns (compound nouns) that are made up of two nouns. Here are some examples:

schoolroom, inkstand, bookcase, workman, passer-by, mother-in-law, fountain pen, attorney-general.

These usually form the plural by changing the most important word into the plural. This major word may be in the last part of the compound, as in:

Singular	*Plural*
inkstand	inkstands
schoolroom	schoolrooms

bookcase	bookcases
workman	workmen
girlfriend	girlfriends
fountain-pen	fountain-pens
classroom	classrooms
breakdown	breakdowns

Or it may be in the first part of the compound, as in:

Singular	*Plural*
court-martial	courts-martial
passer-by	passers-by
grant-in-aid	grants-in-aid
notary public	notaries public
attorney-general	attorneys-general
brother-in-law	brothers-in-law

But a very few have plurals in both parts, as in:

Singular	*Plural*
man friend	men friends
woman pilot	women pilots
woman driver	women drivers
man student	men students

But contrast this last group with

male student	male students
lady driver	lady drivers

which are not really compound nouns, but single nouns accompanied by adjectives.

Exercises

A Make the following sentences plural:

1 There is a deer on the hill-side.
2 This sheep has white wool; that sheep has black wool.
3 The bookcase is made of mahogany.
4 I am going to pay the workman.
5 My son-in-law is coming to visit me.
6 It is difficult to get a woman driver who will drive a taxi.
7 A sheep is eating the vegetable in my garden.
8 I have asked my sister-in-law to come shopping with me.
9 The classroom is being swept.
10 A passer-by found the lost key.

B Put in the missing verbs (is, are, was, were) in the following sentences. Say what number each verb is. No. 1 is done for you.

1 The boy's trousers ______ torn.
Answer: The boy's trousers were torn (plural).
2 There ______ some bad news in the paper this morning.
3 His clothes ______ made by a good tailor.
4 That furniture ______ very expensive.
5 The advice that he gave me ______ good.
6 The people in that room ______ waiting for me.
7 My scissors ______ not very sharp.
8 This information ______ just what I want.
9 All the fish in the pond ______ swimming about.

4 Possessive Adjectives (1)

Revision (Book 1, pages 25 to 30). Adjectives go with nouns (generally standing before the noun) and tell us something about them. There are adjectives of quality ('what sort?'), quantity ('how many?'), demonstrative adjectives ('pointing out') and interrogative adjectives ('asking questions').

Possessive Adjectives

This is *my* cat.

That is *your* cat.

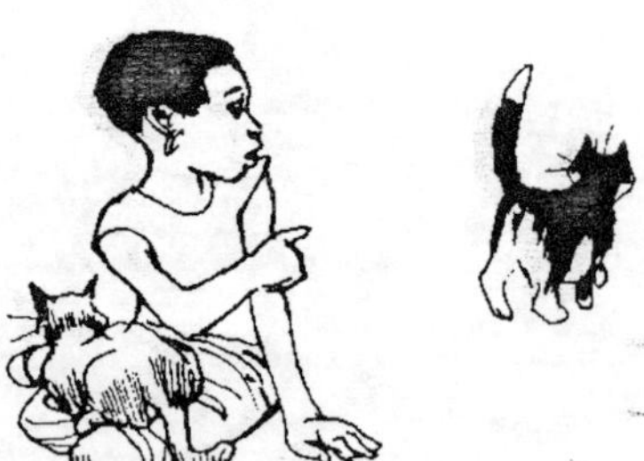

Look at *his* cat.

Look at *her* cat.

Have you seen *our* cat?

Their cat is up the tree.

In all these sentences you will notice that there are words that show to whom those various cats belong.

my cat, *your* cat, *his* cat, and so on.

These words (all going with the noun *cat*) are adjectives; and because they show 'possession', we call them **Possessive Adjectives**. Let us collect them and arrange them like this:

POSSESSIVE ADJECTIVES

	Singular	Plural
1st Person	my	our
2nd Person	your	your
3rd Person	his, her, its	their

Exercises

A In each of the blank spaces in the following, write the possessive adjective and the personal pronoun (objective case) that corresponds to the possessor. The first one is done for you.

I have a book.	This is <u>my</u> book. I have brought it with <u>me</u>.
You have a book.	This is ______ book. You have brought it with ______ .
He has a book.	This is ______ book. He has brought it with ______ .
She has a book.	This is ______ book. She has brought it with ______ .

It (the dog) has a bone.	This is ______ bone. It has brought it with ______ .
We have a book.	This is ______ book. We have brought it with ______ .
They have a book.	This is ______ book. They have brought it with ______ .

B In the following sentences replace the word in italics by a possessive adjective: (You have to re-arrange the words in Nos. 6, 8, 9 and 10)

1. The mother told *the mother's* little girl a story.
2. Tom rode *Tom's* bicycle to school.
3. The little bird built *the little bird's* nest in the tree.
4. Susan made a dress for *Susan's* doll.
5. The teacher told Richard to bring *Richard's* book to the desk.
6. I have lost the pen-knife *that belongs to me.*
7. Mr and Mrs Antia have just gone into *Mr and Mrs Antia's* house.
8. We have sold the car *that belonged to us.*
9. The dog has hurt the paw *that is the dog's.*
10. I want the book *that belongs to me*, not the book *that belongs to you.*

5 Possessive Adjectives (2)

You have learned what the possessive adjectives are. Now we must notice three points about the way they behave.

1 **The singular forms, i.e. *my, your, his, her, its* are used if the *possessor* is singular.** It doesn't matter whether the thing that is possessed is singular or plural.

A few examples will make the matter quite clear.

Let us take the possessive adjective *my*, which is of course singular, and put a singular noun with it.

my sister.

Now we will use a plural noun with it.

my sisters.

In some languages, when the noun is plural, the possessive adjective is plural too. In English it isn't. Here are some more examples.

my { pocket is full of nuts. / pockets are full of nuts.

his { book is on the table. / books are on the table.

her { friend is coming to visit her. / friends are coming to visit her.

your { window is broken. / windows are broken.

2 **The plural forms, i.e. *our, your, their* are used if the *possessor* is plural.** It doesn't matter whether the thing possessed is singular or plural, e.g.

Our cat (*singular*) is in the house.

Our cats (*plural*) are in the house.

I have just been talking to your brother (*singular*).
I have just been talking to your brothers (*plural*).
They are walking with their son (*singular*).
They are walking with their sons (*plural*).

Have you noticed that 'your' (like 'you') can be either singular or plural form?

3 *His* is masculine, *her* is feminine. *My, your, our, their* are used for masculine or feminine. *Its* is used for neuter gender singular; *their* is used for neuter gender plural.

If the possessor is masculine gender the possessive adjective is masculine. If the possessor is feminine, the possessive adjective is feminine. It doesn't matter which gender the thing possessed is. For example:

She is feeding her cat.
He is feeding his cat.
The tree is losing its leaves.

Miama is walking with her mother.
Timi is walking with his mother.
Jumai is walking with her father.
The mother is walking with her son.

The father is walking with his daughter.
Mulikat is carrying her brother.
Dele is carrying his sister.

And here you can see all these uses of the possessive adjectives.

I have a name; my name is Timi.
You have a name; your name is Gogo.
She has a name; her name is Uyi.
It has a name; its name is Jumbo.
We have a name; our name is Dikko.
You have a name; your name is Nwosu.
They have a name; their name is Ankrah.

Exercises

A Make sentences of your own, using
my, your, his, her, its, our, their.

B Here is a short story. Rewrite it, putting possessive adjectives in the blank spaces and in place of the words in italics.

Roadside Vendors

There are many different kinds of roadside vendors along the busy streets of Lagos. On any day, along *the busy streets'* congested sides, you will find seated women selling *the women's* wares, little girls with bottles of cold drinks in bowls on *the little girls'* heads. Here there is a little boy with *the little boy's* pile of plastic balls in front of him, there a newspaper vendor hurrying along advertising *the newsvendor's* newspapers.

'Madam, won't you buy ______ little son this fine toy?' asks a toy seller.
'______ little son is eighteen years old!' she says, walking on.
Plate sellers don't usually shout *the plate sellers'* wares; they sit quietly and wait for customers to approach *the plate sellers'* stalls.

The problem about buying a roadside article is how to judge *the article's* reliability. You cannot test the article before buying it as you can in a shop. Parts of it may be missing when you open the carton, or *the article's* instructions may be in Japanese or Hungarian.

Then, when you get the article home, you are not even sure of ______ performance. A man once found that *the man's* electric kettle, bought hastily at the roadside, could not be used as ______ connecting cord had not been included in the carton. ______ wife lost ______ temper and would have quarrelled with him but for the presence of ______ two little sons.

Finally, the roadside purchase does not necessarily have the advantage of a low price. Tinu once bought a radio cassette for ______ car, only to discover next day that the car parts shop was selling it at a lower price.

So, according to ______ uncle, in Lagos you have to be on the alert, or you and ______ money will soon be parted.

6 Comparison of Adjectives

Mr Bingo Mr Jingo Mr Stingo

Mr Bingo is a *strong* man. Mr Jingo is *stronger.* Mr Stingo is the *strongest* man of the three.

Mr Bingo, Mr Jingo and Mr Stingo have different degrees of strength and, as you will notice, we show that by three different forms of the adjective:

strong stronger strongest

In Grammar these three forms are called the **Positive** degree, the **Comparative** degree and the **Superlative** degree.

A great many adjectives form their comparative degree by adding *er*, and their superlative by adding *est*, to the positive.

e.g.

Positive	*Comparative*	*Superlative*
tall	taller	tallest
short	shorter	shortest
quick	quicker	quickest
old	older	oldest

Sometimes the last letter of the positive is doubled, e.g.

Positive	*Comparative*	*Superlative*
hot	hotter	hottest
fat	fatter	fattest
big	bigger	biggest
thin	thinner	thinnest

If the positive ends in 'e' we only add 'r' and 'st', e.g.

large	larger	largest
fine	finer	finest

Adjectives that end in 'y' usually change this to 'i' in the comparative and superlative, e.g.

pretty	prettier	prettiest
happy	happier	happiest
heavy	heavier	heaviest

Exercises

A What are the three degrees of Comparison?

B Give the Comparative and the Superlative of the following adjectives:

high, long, bright, new, hot, mad, thin, red, happy, lazy.

7 Comparison of Adjectives (2)

You have just seen one way in which adjectives form their Comparative and Superlative; they add *er* and *est* to the Positive.

Some adjectives form their comparative and superlative by using 'more' and 'most', e.g.

This is an exciting book.	This is a *more* exciting book.	This is the *most* exciting of all.

The adjectives that do this are usually rather long words. All adjectives of three or more syllables, e.g. ex-cit-ing, in-ter-est-ing, un-for-tu-nate, are compared like this.

Here are some further examples.

Positive	*Comparative*	*Superlative*
important	more important	most important
dangerous	more dangerous	most dangerous
valuable	more valuable	most valuable
wonderful	more wonderful	most wonderful
convenient	more convenient	most convenient

Irregular Comparison

You will find, over and over again, that when you get some rule in English grammar, there are always some exceptions, some disobedient words that won't obey the rules. Well, there are one or two exceptions to these rules for Comparison of Adjectives. Take 'good' for example. We can't say 'gooder' and 'goodest' any more than we can say 'badder' and 'baddest' or 'littler' and 'littlest'. We'll just gather these 'disobedient' words together and call them the Irregular Comparatives and Superlatives

Positive	*Comparative*	*Superlative*
many fish	more fish	most fish

little food	less food	least food

Positive	Comparative	Superlative
good	better	best
bad	worse	worst
far	{ farther / further	{ farthest / furthest
much	more	most

There are just three other important things for you to notice.

1 With the positive degree we use *as* before the adjective and *as* after it, e.g.

This stick is *as* long *as* this one.

(With the negative some people use *so* . . . *as*, e.g.

'This stick is not *so* long *as* this one,'

but in ordinary speech *as* . . . *as* is more usual.)

2 With the Comparative we use *than* after the adjective, e.g.

This stick is longer *than* that one.
This horse is better *than* that one.
He has more money *than* I have.

3 After the Superlative we often use *of*, e.g.

This is the sharpest *of* the three knives.
That is the prettiest *of* her dresses.

Exercises

A Give the Comparative and the Superlative of the following:

strong, merry, wide, dangerous, difficult, good, fortunate, bad, useful, nice, little, beautiful, far, greedy, much, magnificent, many.

B Fill in the missing words:

1 Timi is older ______ Rufai.
2 Folu is not ______ old ______ Timi.
3 Timi is ______ oldest ______ the three.
4 This book is better ______ that.
5 This book is not ______ good ______ that.
6 This book is ______ best ______ the three.
7 That exercise is more difficult ______ this one.
8 The weather is worse today ______ it was yesterday.
9 It was not ______ bad yesterday ______ it is today.
10 Today's weather is ______ worst ______ the week.

C Write out these sentences putting the adjectives that are in brackets into their correct form. (One or two are already in the correct form. Leave them as they are.)

1 Ayi is (old) than Kweku.
2 Khama is the (clever) boy in the class.

3 The weather is (fine) today than it was yesterday.
4 Accra is not the (big) city in the world.
5 This sentence is (difficult) than the first one.
6 My dog is as (good) as yours.
7 My dog is (good) than yours.
8 Muri's dog is the (good) of the three.
9 The cat will be much (happy) in her new home.
10 My cold is (bad) today than it was yesterday.
11 This mountain is the (high) in Africa.
12 This piece of homework is as (bad) as your last one.
13 This piece of homework is (bad) than your last one.
14 This piece of homework is the (bad) you have ever done.
15 Rufai is not as (tall) as Timi.
16 Timi is (tall) than Rufai.
17 Timi is the (tall) boy in the class.
18 Luanda is (far) from London than Rome is.
19 Mr Ankrah is (rich) than Mr Nwosu, but I don't think he is (happy) than Mr Nwosu.
20 They have (many) hens than we have, but they get (few) eggs.

D Answer the following questions:

1 Timi is taller than Rufai, and Rufai is taller than Folu. Which of the boys is the tallest? Which is the shortest?
2 It is hotter in Kinshasa than it is in London. It is not as hot in Oslo as it is in London. Which of the three cities is the hottest? Which is the coldest?
3 Rufai got fewer marks than Folu in the examination. Edet got fewer than Rufai. Which boy got most marks? Which boy got fewest?
4 A train goes faster than a ship but not as fast as an aeroplane. Which is the fastest? Which is the slowest?

8 The Articles a, an, the

ABDUL Please, sir, what part of speech is *a* or *an* or *the*?

TEACHER Well, what do you think? What do they always go with? Here are some examples: a book, *an* egg, *the* dog, *the* houses.

ABDUL They always seem to go with nouns.

TEACHER Quite right, they do. So they are . . .?

ABDUL Adjectives.

TEACHER Quite right. They are adjectives, though *the* is sometimes called the definite article and *a* (*an*) the indefinite article.

ABDUL Please, sir, what's the difference between *a* and *an*?

TEACHER Well, here are some examples:

a boy	an umbrella
a house	an ear
a ship	an ink-bottle
a dog	an orange

Now can you tell me the answer?

ABDUL Oh yes, I see it. If the noun begins with a consonant sound, you use *a*, but if it begins with a vowel sound, you use *an*.

TEACHER With words like hour, honourable, honest, we use *an* because the *h* is not sounded. Also, *a* (*an*) originally meant one, e.g.

'Timi has *an* egg' means 'Timi has one egg.'

So can *a* or *an* go with any noun, Folu?

FOLU Oh, no; only if they are singular number.

TEACHER Of course! You can say 'a book' but not 'a books', 'a woman' but not 'a women'. The plural of 'a book' is 'books' or 'some books'. Here are a few examples.

Singular	*Plural*
A horse is a useful animal.	Horses are useful animals.
An orange grows on a tree.	Oranges grow on trees.
There is a book on the table.	There are books (*or* some books) on the table.

A simple way of knowing whether 'a leaf' should change to 'leaves' or 'some leaves' is to first decide whether the 'a' means *one* piece or whether it means that type of article in general, e.g.

There is a tiger behind you *becomes* There are some tigers behind you

but A tiger is a dangerous animal *becomes* Tigers are dangerous animals.

However, in certain circumstances it is correct to make the first sentence plural by saying, 'There are tigers behind you!' So this is a variable rule which you will have to learn more about later.

Now, here's a question for you, Musa:

Can *a* or *an* be used with any singular noun?

MUSA Yes, I should think so.

TEACHER Well, think about it, and in our next lesson we'll see if your answer is right.

Exercises

A Put *a* or *an* before each of the following words:

cat, pen, eye, hour, telephone, aeroplane, horse, ice-cream, umpire.

When do you use *a* and when do you use *an*?

B Make the following sentences plural:

1 A rose is a flower.

2 A mouse is a small animal.
3 There is a horse in the field.
4 Mary gave me a book yesterday.
5 A noun is the name of a thing.
6 There is a mango on the plate.
7 A table is a piece of furniture.
8 A flamboyant is a big tree.
9 A child isn't always careful on the road.
10 You can buy more with a cedi than with a pesewa.

9 Countable and Uncountable Nouns

TEACHER At the end of the lesson yesterday, I asked you whether *a* or *an* could be used with any singular noun. You thought it could, didn't you, Musa?

MUSA Yes, sir, I did. But I've been thinking about it since yesterday and now I am not so sure. I thought of the nouns 'bread' and 'steam'. I wouldn't put *a* or *an* in front of those nouns. So I think the answer to your question is 'no'. But I can't say which nouns can have *a* and which nouns can't.

TEACHER Well done, Musa. You have brought up an interesting but rather difficult point. Listen to this carefuly. **All common nouns can be divided into two classes, countable nouns and uncountable ones.**

Nouns like *eggs, boys, bicycles, aeroplanes*, are countable – that is to say, you can count them. You can have three bicycles, ten boys, twenty aeroplanes, fifty eggs.

But what about things like *water, air, bread, anger, truth, money, wood, smoke, glass, rain*? You would laugh if I said 'Count the *waters* coming out of this tap' or 'How many *airs* are there in this room?' or 'Have you ten *moneys*?' I agree you could, perhaps, count drops of water, slices of bread, or coins. *Drops, slices, coins* are countables, but *water, bread, money* on their own, i.e. without special assisting words for counting, are uncountables. Do you think you see the difference?

MUSA Oh yes, I think so.

RUFAI Please, sir, you said that *glass* was one of the uncountables. But can't I say 'There are three *glasses* on the tray'? So wouldn't *glass* there be a countable?

TEACHER Yes, Rufai, it would. You see, a word in English may often have more than one meaning. If, as in your sentence, *glass* means 'a thing we can drink out of', then it is a countable. But if, as I meant it, *glass* is the stuff that windows are made of, it is an uncountable. In the sentence, 'My house is built of stone,' the word *stone*, the stuff my house is made of, is an uncountable. But if I say, 'The boys threw stones through the window,' well, you could certainly count them! *Stone* there would be a countable. Has that cleared away your difficulty?

RUFAI Oh yes, sir. That's all quite clear.

TEACHER So the rule is:–

You can use *a* (*an*) with *countable* nouns;
you can't use a (*an*) with *uncountable* nouns.

Exercises

A Arrange the following into two columns, countables in column 1, uncountables in column 2.

1	2
Countables	Uncountables

gold, machine, tree, wood, silver, happiness, flower, flour, machinery, steel, spoon, milk, electricity, tea, steam, book, house, rain, cigarette, tobacco, mud, wheel, cotton, teacher, education, butter, hat, shoe, leather, clothing, goodness, grass, pen, paper, ink, penny, corn.

B Copy out these sentences putting *a* or *an* where necessary. Remember that only countables that are singular take *a* or *an*. Don't put anything before each plural countable noun and each uncountable noun.

1 That is ______ man.
2 These are ______ men.
3 ______ house can be built of ______ stone.
4 ______ cow is ______ animal.
5 ______ cows are ______ animals.
6 ______ cigarette is made of ______ tobacco and ______ paper.
7 ______ chair is made of ______ wood.
8 ______ chairs are made of ______ wood.
9 ______ man must have ______ air to live.

10 ______ shrimps live in ______ water.
11 ______ flower grows in ______ garden.
12 ______ flowers grow in ______ gardens.
13 We get ______ milk from ______ cow.
14 We get ______ milk from ______ cows.
15 ______ window is made of ______ glass.
16 ______ rain falls from the sky.
17 ______ shoe is made of ______ leather.
18 ______ shoes are made of ______ leather.
19 ______ grass grows in ______ field.
20 ______ grass grows in ______ fields.
21 ______ gramophone plays ______ music.
22 You put ______ record on ______ gramophone to get ______ music.
23 ______ flour is made from ______ wheat.
24 ______ loaf is made from ______ flour.
25 ______ loaves are made from ______ flour.

C Put these sentences into the singular:

1 Books are on my desk.
2 Roses are flowers.
3 Dogs are animals.
4 Houses are buildings.
5 Chairs are pieces of furniture.
6 Nouns are the names of things.
7 Knives are made of steel.
8 Carpenters work with hammers and saws.
9 Men light cigarettes with matches.
10 Dogs have tails.
11 Jackets are made of cloth.
12 Fishes live in water.
13 Flamboyants are big trees.
14 Soldiers carry rifles.
15 Horses are useful to farmers.
16 Careful pupils are good pupils.
17 Bridges are often made of stone.
18 Children are not always thoughtful.
19 Men can make good meals from rice, yams, meat and plantains.
20 You can buy more with leones than with cents.

D Here is a little story:

The Rain-Doctor

Joe was visiting Nosa whose father had recently died. 'It's a pity I couldn't be at the burial because of my official trip abroad, Nosa. How did it go?'

'Very well indeed, thanks, Joe. It's always a relief to get these traditional affairs over and done with. Papa was very old, his health had been failing. I think he himself felt it was time to join friends of his own age who had departed. So his death was no surprise. We were quite prepared and everything went smoothly. We have a store which sells cement, wood, nails, roofing and other building materials, so we were able to put up temporary sheds for the ceremony quite easily. Colleagues and friends all came to help us give him a rousing send-off. The only worry I had at first was the weather. If it had rained, with those sheds, everything would have been ruined and all our expenditure wasted. But I found a rain-doctor to keep the weather fine for the entire five days. It cost a lot of money, plus his food and beer for the period, (he is forbidden during the ritual to touch water in any form), but it was worth it. The man really knew his job.'

'So it didn't rain from – let's see – that Saturday to the following Wednesday?' asked Joe.

'That's right.'

'And did it remain fine for another three days at least?'

'Yes,' replied Nosa, 'although the rain-doctor had led us to expect a real storm as soon as he withdrew his powers. But how did you know? You weren't here!'

'Well,' said Joe, 'I wish you had mentioned your fears about the weather when I phoned just before my departure. I would have saved you all that money. You remember I left on Friday, the day before the burial. The day before that there was the long-range weather forecast on television, which I always listen to. That Thursday's forecast said very definitely that the weather for the next ten days at least would be hot and completely rainless.'

How many countable and how many uncountable nouns can you pick out from the story?

10 Verbs: Tense

Revision (Book I, pages 34 to 53). Verbs are used to express an action or a state of being. There is always a verb in a sentence. If the subject of a sentence is singular, the verb is singular; if the subject is plural, the verb is plural. Verbs that take objects are called Transitive verbs. Verbs that don't take objects are called Intransitive verbs.

Tense

TEACHER What day *is* it today?
PUPIL Today *is* Tuesday.
TEACHER What day *was* it yesterday?
PUPIL Yesterday it *was* Monday.
TEACHER What day *will* it *be* tomorrow?
PUPIL Tomorrow it *will be* Wednesday.

In these sentences we have been thinking about three different times. The first question and its answer were about the Present time: today.

The second pair were about Past time; yesterday.

The third were about Future time; tomorrow.

Here are some other examples.

FATIMA A This year I *am* in the 2nd Year English Class.
B Last year I *was* in the 1st Year English Class.
C Next year I *shall be* in the 3rd Year English Class.

NAUNA A I *have* a blue dress on today.
B I *had* a green one on yesterday.
C I *shall have* a red one on tomorrow.

TEACHER A This week my pupils *do* their lessons in room number four.
B Last week they *did* them in room number three.
C Next week they *will do* them in room number five.

Sentences A concern the **Present** time: now, this year, this week.
Sentences B concern the **Past** time: last year, yesterday, last week.
Sentences C concern the **Future** time: next year, tomorrow, next week.

As you can see, the verbs have a different form to show these different times.

Present	*Past*	*Future*
am	was	shall be
have	had	shall have
do	did	will do

These different forms are called **Tenses.**

The Present Tense is used for actions taking place in the present.

The Past Tense is used for actions that took place in the past.

The Future Tense is used for actions that will take place in the future.

Here is the Simple Present Tense, the Simple Past Tense and the Simple Future Tense of the verbs *be* and *have.*

Simple Present Tense	*Simple Past Tense*	*Simple Future Tense*
	be	
I am	I was	I shall be
he, she, it is	he, she, it was	he, she, it will be
we are	we were	we shall be
you are	you were	you will be
they are	they were	they will be

have

I have	I had	I shall have
he, she, it has	he, she, it had	he, she, it will have
we have	we had	we shall have
you have	you had	you will have
they have	they had	they will have

Notice that in the future tense we use *shall* in the 1st person (i.e. with *I* and *we*) and *will* with all other persons. This will be explained more fully later.

Exercises

A What do you understand by the tense of a verb? What are the names of the three tenses you have learned so far?

B Write out:

1 the simple present tense;
2 the simple past tense;
3 the simple future tense of the verbs *be* and *have*.

C Put these sentences into the Simple Past Tense. Add a word or phrase to some of them to show past time, e.g. yesterday, last week, until yesterday, two years ago, when I was younger, etc. Miss out a word if necessary, or change any word or phrase which can only be used in the present tense.

1 I am in school.
2 He is a good swimmer.
3 We are in the second-year class.
4 The flowers are very beautiful.
5 I have a new football.
6 Tom has five kobo in his pocket.
7 The sun is very hot.
8 Mary has a new dress.
9 I have a very small pair of shoes.
10 I am Richard's friend.
11 Abu's sheep has a little lamb.
12 This pen is new today.
13 The children are not ready for school.
14 We have plenty of time to get to school.
15 I am very tired after playing football.
16 They are not able to do this exercise.
17 He has never been late for school.

11 Verbs: Tense (2)

do

Simple Present Tense	*Simple Past Tense*	*Simple Future Tense*
I do	I did	I shall do
he, she, it does	he, she, it did	he, she, it will do
we do	we did	we shall do
you do	you did	you will do
they do	they did	they will do

Here are some more sentences using the verbs *be, have, do* in the three tenses.

Present Tense

MIAMA Today *is* my birthday, so I *have* a holiday today. On my birthday I always *do* my work early in the morning so that I *am* free for the rest of the day. This year my birthday *is* on a Tuesday. I *have* a present for my birthday, here it *is* in my hand. I *am* eleven years old today.

Past Tense

JUMAI It *was* my birthday yesterday, so I *had* a holiday then. I *did* my work early in the morning so that I *was* free for the rest of the day. My birthday *was* on a Monday. I *had* a present for my birthday; it *was* a digital watch. I *was* twelve years old yesterday.

Future Tense

FATIMA It *will be* my birthday tomorrow, so I *shall have* a holiday then. I *shall do* my work early in the morning so that *I shall be* free for the rest of the day. My birthday *will be* on a

Wednesday this year. I *shall have* a party and I know that my mother and father *will give* me a birthday present. I *shall be* thirteen years old tomorrow.

The Tense of a verb shows the time (present, past or future) when the action takes place, took place, or will take place.

Exercises

A Put these sentences into the Simple Present Tense. Change words, add them, or leave them out where necessary.

1 He was a good footballer once.
2 We were in school yesterday.
3 The roses were very beautiful last year.
4 I had a book for my birthday.
5 The sun was very hot yesterday.
6 We were in the second class last year.
7 I did my lessons carefully.
8 Elizabeth had a new doll.
9 The class had English three times a week last year.
10 I had a bad cold last week.
11 Harry was tired after the game of football.
12 We were not able to do the difficult exercise.
13 Tom had a puppy like that when he was younger.
14 The children's hands were very dirty.
15 They had never been late for school until yesterday.
16 You were very careless, weren't you?
17 They had plenty of time to get the work done.
18 You had an English lesson with the teacher yesterday, didn't you?
19 Mary was here yesterday, wasn't she?
20 Those boys were your brothers, weren't they?

B Put the following sentences into the Future Tense. Change words where necessary, using, for example, tomorrow, next year, in a few days' time, in five minutes. Remember to use 'shall' with the 1st persons, 'I' and 'we', and 'will' with all other persons.

1 I am twelve years old today.
2 Timi is twelve years old today.
3 We are in the second class this year.

4 You are in the second class this year.
5 You have plenty of time to finish the work.
6 I have plenty of time to finish the work.
7 We have a busy day today.
8 They have a busy time today.
9 I do my work carefully.
10 He does his work carefully.
11 Eze is a good swimmer.
12 It is a fine day today.
13 I am late for school.
14 The two boys are late for school.
15 The mangoes are ripe on the tree.
16 Rufai is able to do this exercise.
17 I am able to do this exercise.
18 He is ready for school now.
19 We are ready for school now.
20 They are ready for school now.

12 Present Continuous Tense

We have just learned that the tense of a verb shows the time of an action; it shows whether it takes place in the present time, the past time or the future time.

But the tense can also show whether the action is finished or not. For example, look at these sentences:

I *am writing* on the blackboard.
You *are learning* grammar.
Tom *is reading* his book.
The flower *is dying.*
We *are singing* 'Ten Green Bottles'.
They *are fighting.*

All those actions are in the present time and they are all still continuing. The writing, learning, reading, singing, fighting are still going on; they are all still continuing. So this tense is called the Present Continuous Tense.

The Present Continuous Tense is used to express an action that is still going on.

It is quite easy to make it. As you see, it consists of two parts. The first part is a form of the present tense of the verb to be (*am, is* or *are*). The second part is the form of the verb that ends in *-ing*, e.g. *learning, reading, singing*. This form is called the **Present Participle**. You can make the present participle of any verb by adding *-ing* to the infinitive. There are, however, a few small points of spelling that you should notice.

1 Verbs that end in a silent e, drop this e when they add -ing, e.g. dance, dancing; write, writing; hope, hoping.

2 Some verbs double the last letter, e.g. stop, stopping; get, getting; hit, hitting; hop, hopping.

3 Verbs ending in ie, change this to y, e.g. lie, lying; die, dying; tie, tying; vie, vying.

The Present Continuous Tense is made by using *am, is* or *are*, with a Present Participle except for the verbs *can, shall, may, must* and *ought* which have no present participle.

Exercises

A Write down the Present Participle of the following verbs:
walk, sing, talk, eat, dance, write, hope, run, dig, swim, offer, try, reply, die, lie.

B Write out the Present Continuous Tense of the verbs:
speak, take, cut, play, tie.

C Change the following sentences from the Simple Present Tense to the Continuous Present Tense. Add a word or phrase like *now, today, at this moment, at present*, to each sentence.

1 I write a letter.
2 Ifeoma walks to school.
3 We live in that house.
4 My father works in his garden.
5 The book lies on the table.
6 The train stops at the station.
7 We travel to school.
8 The gardener cuts down a tree.
9 Olu comes home.
10 The shopkeeper ties up the parcel.

13 Past Continuous Tense

Sometimes we want to speak of an action that was going on or continuing in the past time. In that case we use the **Past Tense** of the verb *to be* with the Present Participle. Compare the Present Continuous and the Past Continuous, e.g.

Present Continous. We *are having* an English lesson now.
Past Continuous. This time yesterday, we *were having* an English lesson.

Here are some other examples of the Past Continuous Tense.

A year ago I *was living* in Ankara.
I saw Chuka at the station this morning.
Yes, he *was waiting* for Ada, who *was coming* home from Bakori.

Here is the Past Continuous Tense of the verb to go:

Singular	Plural
I was going	we were going
he, she, it, was going	you were going
	they were going

The Past Continuous Tense is very often used to show that an action was going on (or continuing) at a time when something else happened. An example will make that clear. Let's take an action that was still continuing, e.g.

'As I *was coming* to school this morning . . .'

Then something happened:

'I *saw* a car run into a bus.'

Notice that the thing that suddenly happened is expressed by the Simple Past Tense (saw).

Here are some further examples:

Past Continuous (action going on)	Simple Past (for new action)
The teacher *was giving* us a lesson,	when a little dog *walked* into the room.
While we *were having* supper,	all the lights *went* out.
The fire *was still burning*,	when I *passed* the house the next day.
While the man *was looking* in the shop window,	the thief *picked* his pocket.

Sometimes the sentences may be the other way round, i.e. we may mention the new action first, before mentioning the old action that was going on, e.g.

Simple Past	Past Continuous
All the lights *went* out,	while we *were having* supper.
When I *passed* the house next day,	the fire *was* still *burning*.
Harry *did* his homework,	while the other boys *were playing* football.

Exercises

A Write out the Past Continuous Tense of the verbs

do, rise, stop.

B Change the following from Simple Present Tense to Past Continuous Tense.

1 She helps me.

2 A friend plays the piano.

3 We listen to the music.

4 You make a lot of mistakes.
5 The farmer works in the field.
6 The small boy rings the bell.
7 He looks at the pictures.
8 The workman paints the house.

C Change the following sentences from Simple Past Tense to Past Continuous Tense.

1 I swept the floor.
2 The cat slept.
3 The boys wrote a letter.
4 We sang a song.
5 I hoped you would come.
6 Thomas made a model aeroplane.
7 The bell rang.
8 Nosa and Osita swam in the river.

D Put the verb in brackets into the Past Continuous form.

1 John got off the train while it (move).
2 It (rain) when we went out.
3 I (play) the piano when he came into the room.
4 I came into the room when Mary (play) the piano.
5 John (work) all day yesterday.
6 She (live) in England when the War began.
7 He hurt his foot while he (climb) the tree.
8 The baby (eat) its dinner when I came home.
9 He (walk) home when the rain began.
10 The car hit a tree while it (travel) at 60 miles an hour.

E Put in the correct Past Tense of the verbs in these sentences:

1 He (write) a letter when I (see) him.
2 Harry (do) his work while his brothers (play) games.
3 The man (fall down) as he (run) for the bus.
4 We (sing) a song when George (come) into the room.
5 While the teacher (give) a lesson, a small dog (walk) into the room.
6 When the phone (ring), I (work) in the garden.
7 My hat (blow) off while I (cross) the bridge.
8 The rain (begin) to fall while we (watch) the game.
9 Just as I (get) interested in my work, I (have) to go home.
10 He (lose) his wallet while he (struggle) to get on the bus.

14 Simple Present Tense and Present Continuous Tense

PUPIL Please, sir, I don't know when to use the Simple Present Tense and when to use the Present Continuous Tense. Is there any difference between

'Mary plays the piano'

and

'Mary is playing the piano'?

or

'You write on the blackboard'

and

'You are writing on the blackboard'?

TEACHER That is a very good question. I am glad you asked me that. I'll try to make it clear.

The Present Continuous Tense is the one that most truly expresses an action in the present time, an action that is taking place now.

'Mary is playing the piano' or 'I am writing on the blackboard' means that these actions are going on at this very moment.

The Simple Present Tense is generally used for an action that is done regularly, for an action that happens, perhaps, every day. So you often find words like *usually, generally, every day, sometimes, always,* etc., used with it.

I am going to school
PRESENT CONTINUOUS

I go to school every day
SIMPLE PRESENT

Now here is a short composition that Ali Traore wrote for me that will show you the use of the Simple Present Tense. I'll read it to you.

My Daily Programme by Ali Traore

I usually *wake up* every day about six o'clock. I *get* out of bed and *go* and *waken* Musa and Rikku. I sometimes *pull* the covering off them to wake them. Then they *get* up and we *dash* to the bathroom. We *bathe, brush* our teeth and then we *go* back to the bedroom to dress. Mother generally *calls* upstairs, 'Come on boys, breakfast is ready.' So we *hurry* downstairs. We *say*, 'Good morning, Mother,' 'Good morning, Father,' and *sit* down to breakfast. Father *goes* to the office at half-past seven, but before he *goes*, he usually *stops* in front of the mirror and *combs* his hair once more. We *eat* our breakfast and *leave* the table. Then we *go* and *get* our books and school caps. We *say* good-bye to mother, *take* out our bicycles and *cycle* to school.

As you see, all those verbs are in the Simple Present Tense because Ali is telling you his daily habits. He is telling you what he does every day, not what he is doing at that moment.

The Simple Present Tense is used for a repeated or habitual action.

The Present Continuous Tense is used for an action that is still going on.

There are one or two small, but rather important, points that you should notice. In the Simple Present Tense the 3rd person singular usually ends in *s*, e.g.

1st Person Singular	*3rd Person Singular*
I sit	he sit*s*
I get	he get*s*
I read	he read*s*

Sometimes the 3rd person singular ends in *es*, e.g.

I wash	he wash*es*
I go	he go*es*

Sometimes it changes from *y* to *ies*, e.g.

I try	he tr*ies*
I cry	he cr*ies*

Exercises

A Write out the Simple Present Tense of the following verbs: get, sit, catch, smash, go, do.

B Change the following from 1st person singular to 3rd person singular (remember to use both 'he' and 'she')

1 I like chocolate.
2 I write an exercise.
3 I know the answer.
4 I try to do my work well.
5 I wash my face after siesta.
6 I eat my breakfast.
7 I brush my teeth.
8 I say good morning to my mother.
9 I go to school on my bicycle.
10 I do my work carefully.
11 I can speak English.
12 I will help you.
13 I may come here tomorrow.
14 I must finish my work.
15 I ought to be more careful.

C In the following sentences the verbs have been left out. Some of the verbs ought to be in the Present Simple Tense, others in the Present Continuous Tense. Rewrite the sentences putting in the verbs. (The verb to use is given in brackets).

1 (play) Elizabeth ______ the piano well.
She ______ it now.
2 (drive) My father ______ to his office every day.
He ______ there now.
3 (rain) It ______ today.
It usually ______ in July.

4 (speak) He generally ______ Edo, but he ______ English today.
5 (cook) Mother ______ yam in the kitchen just now.
She usually ______ yam for breakfast.
6 (set) The sun ______ in the West.
It ______ now, and soon it will be dark.
7 (sew) My sister always ______ the dresses for her doll.
She ______ one now.
8 (ring) The telephone ______ again.
It sometimes ______ twenty times a day.
9 (do) Sule ______ his homework now.
He usually ______ it in the evening.
10 (sit) (read) (chew) 'What is your father doing?' 'He ______ in an armchair ______ his paper and ______ a kolanut.'
11 (go) Richard ______ to school every day.
12 (learn) In our class today we ______ about the tenses of verbs.
13 (do) Careless students never ______ their work well.
14 (write) 'What is the teacher doing?' 'He ______ on the blackboard.
15 (live) That fat man ______ next door to us.
(go) He is just ______ in at the front door.
16 (spend) We ______ a short holiday in Mamfe.
(go) We ______ there almost every year.
17 (strike) Listen, the clock ______. Count the strokes.
18 (go) (give) Whenever we ______ to my aunt's house she always ______ us some food.
19 (smoke) (see) (smoke) Mr Nwosu ______ too much. Every time I ______ him he is ______.

D *Revision Exercise on Tenses of Verbs*

Here is a story. Some of the verbs should be in the Simple Present, some in the Simple Past, some in the Past Continuous and some in the Future Tense. Rewrite it putting the verbs in the right tenses.

Don't Read Only the Headlines, Timi – Part 2

'Now that you (know) the full story,' (say) Timi's father, 'can you understand why the newspaper editor (use) headlines instead of full sentences?'

Timi (answer), 'I (think) he (want) to save space so that the paper can accept more advertisements and include more news items in its columns.'

'Exactly,' (agree) Timi's father. 'Also, the editor and his staff (want) the paper's major stories to attract as much attention as possible, so as to sell plenty of copies. Headlines with big, bold letters usually (attract) buyers who (want) to satisfy their curiosity by reading the full story. But if you (increase) the size of the words, you have to reduce their number, otherwise the story heading alone (fill) the whole page. Take this Bank story headline; the full sentence would probably be: 'The United National Bank of Iba (hold) two dances which (last) all night because the dancers (be) unable to return to their homes before day-break.'

'Thank you, Papa,' (say) Timi. 'I (understand) now.' He (think) for a moment further and (add), 'Perhaps also the editor sometimes (want) to puzzle readers by using short headlines which (be) difficult to understand if one (do) not read the full story?'

'Yes,' (reply) his father. 'That sometimes (happen). One day I (hurry) to the office and as I (drive) past the newsvendors at Independence Square I (see) a startling headline. I (stop) so suddenly that the car which (be) behind me and which (try) to overtake very nearly (run) into me. That (show) how arresting headlines sometimes (be). The same thing (apply) to book titles and cinema film titles. Now, what have you learnt from this discussion, Timi? What you (do) in future?'

'In future I (read) the full story before I (decide) what the headline or title (mean).'

15 Negative of Verbs The Peculiars

There are two principal ways in which verbs can form their negatives. Let's call them Method A and Method B.

Method A

There are only a few verbs that use this method but they are verbs that are used very often.

They are a strange little group; they don't behave like other verbs in a number of ways and so they are sometimes called the *Peculiars*. We shall be talking about their odd ways quite often, so we may as well have a list of them.

There are only twelve of them in all and, for the moment, we are only going to consider eight of them. They are:

be (*am, is, are, was, were*) *have* (*has, had*), *can* (*could*), *shall* (*should*), *will* (*would*), *may* (*might*), *must, ought.*

The others, which we will consider later, are *do* (*does, did*) *need, dare* and *used to.*

The Peculiars form their negative simply by adding *not*.

And they are the only verbs out of the thousands of English verbs that make their negative in that way, (the way we have called Method A).

Here are some examples:

Affirmative	*Negative*
He is English.	He is *not* English.
I have seen him.	I have *not* seen him.
She can speak English.	She can*not* speak English.
We shall have a lesson tomorrow.	We shall *not* have a lesson tomorrow.
I will write a letter.	I will *not* write a letter.
You may have another banana.	You may *not* have another banana.
You must write in your book.	You must *not* write on the wall.
Timi ought to do his own work.	He ought *not* to ask Jem to do it for him.

Contractions

These negatives are often shortened, especially in conversation. Here are the contracted (shortened) forms:

Negative	Contracted Form	Negative	Contracted Form
is not	isn't	will not	won't
are not	aren't	shall not	shan't
have not	haven't	must not	mustn't
has not	hasn't	ought not	oughtn't
cannot	can't		

'Have' is rather confusing because it has two forms, the peculiar form, which assists other verbs, and the normal form which stands on its own, e.g. 'We have a house' and behaves like other verbs. Because of its dual nature, you will come across short questions: 'Have you a ruler?' and shortened negatives: 'He hadn't a ruler' where the normal verb is treated like a peculiar. This is found more often in conversation than in writing or in formal speech, where the normal forms 'Do you have a ruler?' and 'He didn't have a ruler' are more acceptable. 'Do' and 'be' also have dual functions like 'have'.

Exercises

A How many Peculiars are there? Name the eight we have just discussed. How do they all make the negative?

B Write down the shortened forms of:

1 is not.	**2** ought not	**3** are not.
4 must not.	**5** have not.	**6** has not.
7 will not.	**8** cannot.	**9** shall not.

C Make the following sentences negative:

1. She is a teacher.
2. I am Kenyan.
3. We have done our homework.
4. You are my pupils.
5. We are your pupils.
6. He has torn my English book.
7. They have met the new teacher.
8. Rufai can swim very well.
9. I shall go to see him tomorrow.
10. You ought to write your exercise in this book.
11. I will do what you ask me.
12. You must go now.

16 Negative of Verbs The Peculiars (2)

You have already had the Past Tense of some of the Peculiars, e.g.

Present Tense	Past Tense	Present Tense	Past Tense
am (is)	was	have (has)	had
are	were	do (does)	did

Here is the past tense of some of the others.

Present	Past	Present	Past
can	could	will	would
shall	should	may	might

Must and *ought* have only the one form. These verbs will be discussed more fully in Book 3. The negative of these past tenses of the Peculiars is often shortened, especially in conversation. Here are the contracted or short forms:

Negative	Short Form	Negative	Short Form
was not	wasn't	should not	shouldn't
had not	hadn't	would not	wouldn't
could not	couldn't	might not	mightn't

The Past Tense negative of the Peculiars is made, just as the Present Tense is, simply by adding *not*, e.g.

Affirmative	*Negative*
He was here yesterday.	He was *not* (wasn't) here yesterday.

I had read your letter.	I had *not* (hadn't) read your letter.
John could swim when he was six.	John could *not* (couldn't) swim when he was six.
You should always say what you think.	You should *not* (shouldn't) always say what you think.
He said that he might come.	He said that he might *not* (mightn't) come.
She said that she would help us.	She said that she would *not* (wouldn't) help us.

Exercises

A Write down the shortened forms of:

1 was not. **2** might not. **3** had not.
4 would not. **5** should not. **6** could not.

B Make the following sentences negative:

1 Gogo was at our house last night.
2 They had built a shed behind their house.
3 John could swim when he was three years old.
4 Your friends were at the party last night.
5 He would go there if I went.

C Put the following sentences into the Past Tense:

1 I can see the car in the distance.
2 We shall go if we are asked.
3 He will help us if he can.
4 He says that he will come to the party. (*Begin* 'He said . . .')
5 She thinks she may finish her work by seven o'clock. (*Begin* 'She thought . . .')

17 Negative of Verbs Continuous Tense

You remember, of course, that the Continuous Tense is formed by using parts of one of the Peculiars (the verb *to be*) with the Present Participle. So the Continuous Tenses form their negative, as the Peculiars do, simply by adding *not*. For example:

Present Continuous Tense

Affirmative	*Negative*
I am writing on the blackboard.	I am *not* writing on the blackboard.
You are learning English.	You are *not* (aren't) learning English.
Timi is reading his history book.	Timi is *not* (isn't) reading his history book.
We are living in the twentieth century.	We are *not* (aren't) living in the eighteenth century.
Tomi is coming to see us this afternoon.	Tomi is *not* (isn't) coming to see us this afternoon.

Past Continuous Tense

The negative of the Past Continuous Tense is formed in just the same way, i.e. by adding *not* to the Affirmative. Here are some examples:

Affirmative	*Negative*
When I looked at the baby, it was sleeping.	When I looked at the baby, it was *not* (wasn't) sleeping.
He was working when I saw him.	He was *not* (wasn't) working when I saw him.
They were singing a Kikuyu song.	They were *not* (weren't) singing a Kikuyu song.

Exercises

A Make the following sentences negative. Use contracted forms except in Nos 2 and 8.

1 We are listening to the teacher.
2 I am writing on the blackboard.
3 You are learning English grammar.
4 It is raining hard now.
5 He is going to the cinema.
6 The horses are running very fast.
7 Mary is helping her mother to cook.
8 I am working very hard at present.
9 Tom's brother is coming to the party.
10 You are singing very well today.

B In the following sentences make the verb in the Continuous Tense negative. Use short forms.

1 The horses were running very fast.
2 They were pulling a very heavy load.
3 This time yesterday we were sitting here.
4 Yesterday, the man was watering the garden.
5 It was raining hard when I came to school.
6 When I came to school, it was raining hard.
7 The boys were swimming when we saw them.
8 When we saw them, the boys were swimming.
9 You were working hard when I called.
10 When I called, you were working hard.

18 Interrogative of Verbs: Present Tense and Past Tense

Method A

You saw that the Peculiars were different from other verbs in the way they make their negative. Well, they are different, too, in the way they make their interrogative or question form.

They do it by **inversion**, that is, by putting the verb before its subject, like this:

Statement	*Question*
He (*subject*) is (*verb*) a teacher.	Is (*verb*) he (*subject*) a teacher?
It (*subject*) is (*verb*) ten o'clock.	Is (*verb*) it (*subject*) ten o'clock?

His name is Ali Traore.	Is his name Ali Traore?
You have seen him.	Have you seen him?
She will help us.	Will she help us?
He can speak English.	Can he speak English?
They must go home now.	Must they go home now?
They are working hard.	Are they working hard?

They can't understand the lesson.	Can't they understand the lesson?
He mustn't open the box.	Mustn't he open the box?

The Past Tense Interrogative of the Peculiars is made, just as the Present Tense Interrogative is, by changing round the position of the subject and its verb, e.g.

Statement	*Question*
He was here yesterday.	Was he here yesterday?
You had just read the letter.	Had you just read the letter?
John could swim when he was six years old.	Could John swim when he was six years old?
They were working hard when you saw them.	Were they working hard when you saw them?

The twelve Peculiars are the only verbs that form their interrogatives by inversion.

Exercise

Change the following statements into questions. Don't forget the question-mark (?) at the end of your sentence; also note that each question should begin with its Peculiar verb.

1 It is six o'clock.
2 The children are in the house.
3 They have put toys on the table.
4 We shall see the football match.
5 There are boys and girls in the class.
6 John is sitting in the garden.

7 She has helped her brother.
8 He has found time to do the exercise.
9 I must do the work now.
10 Kofi is very late.
11 They are Greek children.
12 He can go now.
13 She must keep the money.
14 You have sharpened this pencil.
15 I am right.
16 My exercise is right.
17 The girls were afraid of the dog.
18 He can come here tomorrow.
19 Kofi's sister was with him.
20 I must tell him what I did.
21 The children are sleeping.
22 The children were sleeping.
23 The children have slept well.
24 The boys were looking at the picture.
25 The boys are looking at the picture.
26 The boys have looked at the picture.
27 The boys can look at the picture.
28 The boys must look at the picture.
29 The boys can't look at the picture.
30 The boys mustn't look at the picture.

19 Finites and Non-finites

TEACHER You have probably noticed that when we speak of a verb we don't mean just one word. A verb is rather like a family; it has several forms which it can take according to the different types of work it has to do, just as we have different names – father, mother, son, uncle, etc. – for members of a family according to each person's position.

Most verbs have either five forms or four forms. The verbs known as strong verbs (you will learn more about them later) have five forms because they have one form for the past tense and another form for the past participle, e.g. *gave*, (has) *given*. But the verbs known as weak verbs have only four forms, because they use the same form for both the past tense and the past participle, e.g. *walked*, (has) *walked*. The majority of English verbs are now in this group (and a few which were originally strong are joining them and becoming weak), therefore the verbs with four forms are now the commonest. This is probably why these verbs are now also known as regular verbs, whereas the strong verbs with five forms are known as irregular verbs.

Apart from the 5–form and 4–form verbs, a very small number have three forms (e.g. *put, cut*); another small number

have only two forms (e.g. *can*); and *must* has only one form – it never changes!

At the other end is the most irregular of the irregular verbs (and yet the commonest verb in English), the verb *to be*, which has eight forms (*being, were, are, is, been, am, was, to be*); seven of the forms correspond to the five forms of the other irregular verbs, the difference being that the verb *to be* has twin forms *were/was* and *are/am* which are used according to whether the subject is first person singular or first person plural, (no other verb in English does this); the eighth form is the infinitive *to be*, which is distinct and does no other work, whereas in other verbs the form that is used (with 'to') for the infinitive also serves for the present tense of the first and second person singular and plural and the third person plural.

Some forms of the verb can stand alone and make complete sense, while others can't. For example, we can say, quite correctly:

The teacher *gives* us an English lesson,
or The teacher *gave* us an English lesson.

We cannot say, correctly:

The teacher *giving* us an English lesson
or The teacher *given* us an English lesson
or The teacher *to give* us an English lesson.

The forms of a verb that can be used to make a predicate by themselves (i.e. to make sense by themselves) are finite. The forms that cannot make a predicate by themselves are non-finite.

The finites are the simple present tense and the simple past tense of all verbs.

The non-finites are the Present Infinitive, e.g. *to give* (this is the form you will find if you look up the verb in a dictionary), the Present Participle, e.g. *giving*, and the Past Participle, e.g. *given*. The *to* is not a part of the infinitive, but we put it there to show that we are speaking of the whole family.

Comparison of Verb Forms

1. To be	1. To give	1. To walk
2. I am	I give	I walk
3. We are	We give	We walk
You are	You give	You walk
They are	They give	They walk
4. He is	2. He gives	2. He walks
She is	She gives	She walks
It is	It gives	It walks
5. I was	3. I gave	3. I walked
6. We were	We gave	We walked
You were	You gave	You walked
They were	They gave	They walked
7. been	4. given	walked
8. being	5. giving	4. walking

1. To put	______	______
I put	1. I can	1. I must
We put	We can	We must
You put	You can	You must
They put	They can	They must
2. He puts	He can	He must
She puts	She can	She must
It puts	It can	It must
I put	2. I could	
We put	We could	
You put	You could	
They put	They could	
put	______	______
3. putting	______	______

Exercise

A Give the five chief forms of these verbs and say which are finites and which are non-finites:

give, speak, begin, bring, buy, write.

B Give the Present Infinitive, the Present Participle and the Past Participle of these verbs:

fall, know, walk, play, dance, cry, try, come, drink, eat, forget, make, take, bite.

20 Finites and Non-finites (2)

Here is a simple way to tell the difference between finites and non-finites in a sentence.

If there is only one verb word in a simple sentence, it is a finite. If there are two or more, then the first will be a finite and the others will be non-finite. Let us look at one or two examples.

The dog *eats* a bone (only one verb: *finite*).

The dog *ate* a bone (only one verb: *finite*).

The dog *is eating* a bone (two verbs; so *is* is finite, and *eating* is non-finite).

The dog *has eaten* a bone (*has*, finite; *eaten*, non-finite).

The dog *wants to eat* a bone (*wants* finite; *to eat*, non-finite).

Does the dog *eat* bones? (*does*, finite; *eat*, non-finite).

Did the dog *eat* the bones? (*did*, finite; *eat*, non-finite).

Will the dog *eat* the bones? (*will*, finite; *eat*, non-finite).

The dog *is going to eat* the bones (*is*, finite; *going*, non-finite; *to eat*, non-finite).

There is just one other point that I want you to notice about finites and non-finites. The finites change according to the number and person of the subject. The non-finites don't. They never have a subject. For example:

		Finites
1st Person Singular	I	am
2nd Person Singular and Plural	You	are
3rd Person Singular	He	is
1st Person Plural	We	are
3rd Person Plural	They	are

As you see, the finites change. With the first person singular you have *am*, with the second person singular or plural you have *are* and so on.

Now, here are some sentences with finites and non-finites in them. Notice that the finite, *like*, changes, but the non-finite, *to play*, does not, *e.g.*

I like to play games. He likes to play games.

Here is another example. Notice how the finites (*am, are, is, were*) change according to the number and person of the subject; and notice how the non-finite (*learning*) is unchanged.

	Finite	Non-finite	
I	am	learning	English
You	are	learning	English
He	is	learning	English
They	are	learning	English

A finite verb agrees with its subject in number and person.

Exercise

Copy out the following sentences. Then on your paper draw one line under each non-finite and two lines under each finite:

1 The boys are playing football.
2 The boys will play football this afternoon.
3 The boys have played football this afternoon.
4 The boys are going to play football this afternoon.
5 The boys like to play football every afternoon.
6 I am learning English.
7 We are learning to write English.
8 We are going to learn English.
9 John is going to learn to write English.
10 John has learned to write English.
11 Did the boys play football today?
12 Do the boys play football every day?
13 Can you play football?
14 Are you playing football this afternoon?
15 Shall we play football today?
16 Have you played football today?
17 Were the boys playing football today?
18 Is Richard going to play football today?
19 Do you learn to write English?
20 Did you learn to write English?
21 We didn't play football today.
22 They don't play football every day.
23 They haven't played football all afternoon.
24 They were not playing football this afternoon.

21 Past Tense and Past Participle Weak Verbs

We have studied the Past Tense of the Peculiars; now let us look at the other class of verbs. Many of them form their Past Tense and Past Participle by adding *ed, d* or *t* to the Present Tense. These are generally called *weak* or *regular* verbs. Here are some of them.

Present	Past	Present	Past
walk	walked	hope	hoped
open	opened	cry	cried
play	played	pay	paid
want	wanted	lay	laid
stop	stopped	dream	dreamed (*or* dreamt)
dance	danced	burn	burned (*or* burnt)

Note that with some verbs we double the last consonant and many verbs that end in *y* change the *y* to *ied.*

The following sentences will illustrate how the Past Tense and the Past Participle are used.

Present Tense: I *walk* to school every day.
Past Tense: I *walked* to school yesterday.
Past Participle: I have *walked* to school many times.

Present Tense: The man *pays* the workman.
Past Tense: The man *paid* the workman last Saturday.
Past Participle: (i) The man has *paid* the workman every Saturday for two years.
(ii) The workmen are *paid* weekly.

Present Tense: My hens *lay* good eggs.
Past Tense: My hens *laid* six eggs yesterday.

Past Participle: (i) My hens have *laid* twenty eggs since Saturday.

(ii) Seven of the eggs were *laid* on Monday.

As you can see from these examples, the Past Tense and the Past Participle have the same form (*walked, paid, laid*). This is the case with all weak verbs. The majority of English verbs are in this class.

With the Past Participle we generally use part of the verb *to have* or part of the verb *to be*.

Exercises

A How do weak verbs form their Past Tense and Past Participle?

B Give the Past Tense and Past Participle of each of these verbs:

open, talk, cook, wash, stop, drop, cry, dry, pay, say, lay, dream.

22 Past Tense and Past Participle Strong Verbs

You have learned that a number of verbs (the weak verbs) make their Past Tense and Past Participle by adding *d, ed* or *t* to their Present Tense. But there are a number of verbs that don't make their Past Tense and Part Participle like this. Instead, they change their vowel sound and in some cases the end of the word is changed as well. These verbs are called *strong* or *irregular* verbs. Here are a few of the commonest irregular verbs.

Present Tense	Past Tense	Past Participle
begin	began	begun
bite	bit	bitten
blow	blew	blown
break	broke	broken
bring	brought	brought
buy	bought	bought
catch	caught	caught
come	came	come
draw	drew	drawn
drink	drank	drunk
drive	drove	driven
eat	ate	eaten
fall	fell	fallen
fly	flew	flown
forget	forgot	forgotten
get	got	got
give	gave	given
hold	held	held
know	knew	known

Present Tense	Past Tense	Past Participle
lie	lay	lain
mistake	mistook	mistaken
shake	shook	shaken
take	took	taken
think	thought	thought
throw	threw	thrown
wear	wore	worn
win	won	won
write	wrote	written

One verb, *go*, is very irregular. It uses a different word altogether for its Past Tense.

go . went gone

Lie is rather difficult. It is an intransitive verb. Here are three sentences to illustrate its use.

Present Tense: At the beach I often *lie* on the sands and watch the ships sail by.

Past Tense: I *lay* on the sands and watched them yesterday.

Past Participle: After I had *lain* there for an hour or so I went for a swim.

Compare this with the weak verb *lay* (see page 66). *Lay* is a transitive verb. *Lie* is intransitive.

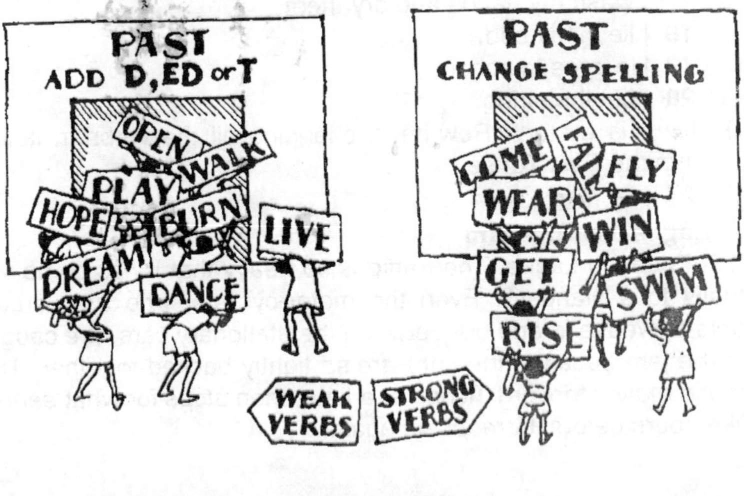

Exercises

A How do strong verbs form their Past Tense and Past Participle?

B Give the Past Tense and Past Participle of each of these verbs and then re-arrange them in two columns, weak verbs in one column and strong verbs in the other:
play, want, stop, buy, drink, eat, write, hope, cry, wear, know, burn, think, fall, come, go, lie, lay, bring.

C Put the following sentences into the Simple Past Tense:

1 I play in the field.
2 He wants to go home.
3 The driver stops the car.
4 He drinks cocoa every day.
5 It begins to rain.
6 They like our house.
7 I dream every night.
8 The teacher gives me a book.
9 He sits at his desk and writes letters.
10 Mimi comes to the class early.
11 We catch fish in the river.
12 The dog eats its dinner.
13 The boys go for a holiday.
14 Rufai knows Gogo.
15 The plane flies very high.
16 He teaches us English.
17 I wash my hands and dry them.
18 I lie in my bed.
19 He goes to school.
20 I cut the string.

D Here is a story. Rewrite it, changing all the verbs in italics into the Past Tense.

A Lagos Traffic-Jam

It *is* Friday in Lagos. The traffic *is* so heavy that it *has* come virtually to a standstill. Even the motor-cyclists, who *are* usually able to weave in and out between the stationary cars, *are* caught in the jam because the cars *are* so tightly packed together. The traffic *moves* forward inches at a time, then *stops* for what *seems* like hours before it *creeps* on again.

The traffic wardens *are* too tired to make any further efforts to direct the traffic, and *watch* idly as cars *form* five or six lanes across the road, or *shoot* out from the side roads and *block* the way for those on the major road.

Suddenly, after a complete blockage, for nearly half-an-hour, at Tinubu Square, the traffic *starts* to move once again. Almost immediately horns *start* blaring from practically every car behind a blue Toyota.

The warden *goes* to investigate the cause of the drivers' impatience, and *finds* that the Toyota driver *is* fast asleep, unaware that the traffic *has* started moving once again.

Instead of being angry, the warden *looks* at the man in admiration and *says* to his colleague that that *is* the only kind of driver who *can* keep his sanity in the Lagos 'go-slow'; he *is* stuck in one spot, and instead of worrying and raising his blood pressure, he quietly *leans* back in his seat and *goes* to sleep!

23 Negative of Verbs Present Tense

You now know Method A, the method of the Peculiars. All verbs except those twelve make their Present Tense negative by the other method, Method B. They do it by using *do* (*does*) and *not.* Here are some examples.

Method B

Affirmative	*Negative*
I know Joseph.	I do not know Joseph.

You know Joseph.	You do not know Joseph.
He knows Joseph.	He does not know Joseph.
We know Joseph.	We do not know Joseph.
They know Joseph.	They do not know Joseph.

There are one or two things that you ought to note here.

1 *Do not* is generally shortened, especially in conversation, to *don't; does not* is generally shortened to *doesn't*.

Here are some other examples. Compare the affirmative and the negative forms of the verb.

Affirmative	*Negative*
Rufai likes ice-cream.	Rufai *doesn't* like ice-cream.
Tam-tam swims well.	Tam-tam *doesn't* swim well.
Grace does the cooking.	Grace *doesn't do* the cooking.

2 Note the *s* in the third person singular.

'He knows Joseph'. There is no *s* on the similar verb in the negative sentence, 'He does not *know* Joseph.'

The part of the verb that is used in the negative (*know, like, swim, do*) is the Infinitive. That is why there is no *s*. Remember lesson 20?

Here are some other examples:

Affirmative	*Negative*
I like learning English.	I *do not* (don't) like learning English.
We come to school on Monday.	We *do not* (don't) come to school on Sunday.
Mr Dikko walks to the office.	Mr Dikko *does not* (doesn't) walk to the office.
They live in London.	They *do not* (don't) live in London.
Rufai swims well.	Rufai *does not* (doesn't) swim well.
That bicycle costs a lot of money.	That bicycle *does not* (doesn't) cost a lot of money.
This plane flies to Entebbe.	This plane *does not* (doesn't) fly to Entebbe.
You know how to do this exercise.	You *do not* (don't) know how to do this exercise.
Nauna works in an office.	Nauna *does not* (doesn't) work in an office.

Exercises

A Give the contracted (shortened) forms of *do not* and *does not*.

B Give the third person singular Simple Present Tense of the following infinitives:

see, know, think, play, eat, drink, learn, sit, write, speak.

C Make the following sentences negative (all are Method B). Use the contracted forms.

1 I know Rufai.

2 We come here every day.

3 You speak English well.
4 They live in London.
5 He knows Rufai.
6 The girl comes here every day.
7 She speaks English well.
8 Rufai lives in Accra.
9 The horse pulls the cart.
10 The horses pull the cart.
11 We swim in the river every day.
12 Obi swims in the river every day.
13 The bird eats the millet.
14 The birds eat the millet.
15 The cat sits on the table.
16 The cats sit on the table.
17 I drink tea every morning.
18 We drink tea every morning.
19 Mr Dikko drinks tea every morning.
20 It rains every day.

D Make the following sentences negative (some are Method A and some are Method B).

1 Dudu bakes a cake.
2 Dudu and Susan bake a cake.
3 Dudu and Susan are baking a cake.
4 The dog chases rabbits.
5 The dogs chase rabbits.
6 The dog is chasing a rabbit.
7 The dogs are chasing a rabbit.
8 That shopkeeper sells good bread.
9 That shopkeeper has good bread.
10 Dudu speaks English well.
11 Dudu can speak English well.
12 Dudu is speaking English now.
13 Taju tries to understand the lesson.
14 Taju is trying to understand the lesson.
15 The boys try to understand the lesson.
16 The boys were trying to understand the lesson.
17 Mr Osifo lives in that house.
18 Mr Osifo is living in that house now.
19 Mr Osifo was living in that house last year.
20 I cycle to school every day.

24 Negative of Verbs Past Tense

The Past Tense negative of all verbs except the Peculiars is made by using *did* and *not* (generally shortened to *n't*) with the present infinitive. Here are some examples:

Affirmative	Negative (Infinitive)
I knew Sule.	I *didn't* know Sule.
You knew Sule.	You *didn't* know Sule.
He knew Sule.	He *didn't* know Sule.
We knew Sule.	We *didn't* know Sule.
They knew Sule.	They *didn't* know Sule.

Affirmative	Negative (Infinitive)
Mr Dada walked to the office.	Mr Dada *didn't* walk to the office.
Uyi opened the door.	Uyi *didn't* open the door.
They paid the money.	They *didn't* pay the money.
Mary broke the glass.	Mary *didn't* break the glass.
Timi bought a bicyce.	Timi *didn't* buy a bicycle.
I wrote a letter.	I *didn't* write a letter.

Here are some more strong verbs (see page 68) with their Past Tense and Past Participle. Learn these.

Present Tense	Past Tense	Past Participle
become	became	become
choose	chose	chosen
dig	dug	dug
fight	fought	fought
find	found	found
forgive	forgave	forgiven
freeze	froze	frozen
grow	grew	grown
hang	hung	hung
ride	rode	ridden
ring	rang	rung
rise	rose	risen
run	ran	run

There is also a weak verb 'hang'. Give its past tense, and its past participle.

Exercises

A Give the Past Tense and Past Participle of the following: (all strong verbs).

run, become, rise, choose, ring, dig, ride, fight, make, find, hang, forgive, lie, freeze, grow, go.

B Make the following sentences negative:

1 I made a mistake in my exercise.
2 The two boys fought in the street.
3 We rode to school on our bicycles.
4 Kodjo forgave the boy who had taken his pencil.
5 I chose these cakes for our party.
6 The water froze in the pond last night.
7 He found the lost ball.
8 My yams grew very well this year.
9 The farmer dug up the cassava.
10 Mr Osifo hung the picture straight.
11 The boy rang the bell.

12 I woke very early this morning.
13 I rose at six o'clock.
14 I got out of bed at six o'clock.
15 The boy ran as fast as he could.
16 John saw that film at the cinema.
17 That baker sold us good bread.
18 The hen laid an egg today.
19 Osama ate her breakfast quickly.
20 You shook the bottle before you took the medicine.
21 He went to school this morning.
22 The children sang very well.
23 We sat on these seats yesterday.
24 Timi spoke French when he was ten years old.
25 The cat sprang on the rat.
26 Every boy stood in his place.
27 Rufai tore that page out of his book.
28 The sun shone brightly this morning
29 He told me the secret.
30 The teacher taught us that rule.
31 The class understood the lesson.
32 The ship sank in the great storm.
33 Kemal swam across the river.
34 The boys went to the party.
35 The thieves stole all the jewels.

25 Interrogative of Verbs: Present Tense

All verbs except the Peculiars form their Present Tense interrogative by using *do* (*does*) and the infinitive. A few examples will make this rule quite clear.

Method B

Statement	Question (Infinitive)
I know Sule.	*Do* I know Sule?
You know Sule.	*Do* you know Sule?
He knows Sule.	*Does* he know Sule?
We know Sule.	*Do* we know Sule?

Statement	Question
You speak English.	*Do* you speak English?
He speaks English.	*Does* he speak English?
That dog bites.	*Does* that dog bite?
Those dogs bite.	*Do* those dogs bite?
I speak clearly.	*Do* I speak clearly?
You come to school every day.	*Do* you come to school every day?
We sing well.	*Do* we sing well?
They play games every day.	*Do* they play games every day?

Exercise

Make the following sentences Interrogative. Don't forget the Question-mark at the end of each of your sentences:

1 Mary likes chocolates.
2 Egypt grows a lot of cotton.
3 That baker sells good bread.
4 I speak English well.
5 He speaks English well.
6 They speak English well.
7 He takes English lessons every day .
8 Alimi swims well.
9 Mary lives in Jos.
10 We buy fruit from the market.
11 You think it will rain today.
12 This book costs twenty five kobo.
13 Mr Dada drives to work every day.
14 The boy tries to understand the lesson.
15 The boys try to understand the lesson.
16 You believe what he says.
17 He writes to his brother every week.
18 They write to their brother every week.
19 The teacher comes to school early.
20 The pupils come to school early.
21 You know the answer.
22 He knows the answer.
23 They learn English at school.
24 She learns English at school.
25 The cat likes milk.
26 You can speak English. *(Be careful! This is different and so are one or two that follow.)*
27 The engine driver sees the signal.
28 The engine driver can see the signal.
29 Mary goes to school every day.
30 Mary is at school today.
31 They sit in their desks for their lesson.
32 The bird sings sweetly.
33 The bird is singing now.
34 John has a new football.
35 John carries his football on to the field.
36 John is carrying his football on to the field.

26 Interrogative of Verbs: Past Tense

All verbs except the Peculiars make their Past Tense interrogative by using *did* and the present infinitive. Here are some examples.

Method B

Statement	Question (Infinitive)
I knew Sule.	Did I know Sule?
You knew Sule.	Did you know Sule?
He knew Sule.	Did he know Sule?
We knew Sule.	Did we know Sule?
They knew Sule.	Did they know Sule?

She walked to school.	Did she walk to school?
He opened the door.	Did he open the door?
They paid the money.	Did they pay the money?
She broke the glass.	Did she break the glass?

Mr Dada drove the car.	Did Mr Dada drive the car?
Timi bought a bicycle.	Did Timi buy a bicycle?
I told you the story.	Did I tell you the story?
He came by aeroplane.	Did he come by aeroplane?
You spoke English.	Did you speak English?

Here are some more strong verbs with their Past Tense and Past Participle. Learn them.

Present Tense	Past Tense	Past Participle
see	saw	seen
sell	sold	sold
shine	shone	shone
sing	sang	sung
sink	sank	sunk
sit	sat	sat
Speak	spoke	spoken
Spring	sprang	sprung
stand	stood	stood
steal	stole	stolen
stick	Stuck	stuck
swim	Swam	swum
teach	taught	taught
tear	tore	torn
Tell	told	told
Understand	understood	Understood
wake	woke	waked or woken

Exercises

A Give the Past Tense and Past Participles of the following verbs:
understand, sell, tell, shake, tear, shine, teach, sing, swim, sink, steal, sit, speak, stand, wake, spring.

B Make the following sentences Interrogative.

1. Mr Dikko walked to his office.
2. The boys tried to understand the lesson.
3. You believed what he said.
4. He wrote to his brother every week.

5 They wrote to their brother every week.
6 The baker sold good bread.
7 The baker burned the bread.
8 The lesson began at nine o'clock.
9 Gogo brought his little brother to school.
10 We bought that fruit from the market.
11 Mr Jaja caught the eight o'clock train.
12 All the boys wore clean uniforms.
13 They thought carefully about that exercise.
14 They all went to the football match.
15 She said she was very busy.
16 Gogo took his little brother to school.
17 His mother made jollof rice for the party.
18 The dog lay in the corner.
19 John held his little brother's hand.
20 Mr Dada went to the office by car.
21 The cruel driver hit the horse.
22 Obi gave his bicycle to his younger brother.
23 The children got a lot of presents at Christmas.
24 Sule forgot to bring his book to the class.
25 The birds flew out of the cage.
26 Gogo's little brother came to school with him.
27 Rufai caught the ball.
28 Rufai fell while he was running.
29 The greedy boy ate all the food.
30 The cat drank its milk.
31 Okon drew a picture of the teacher.
32 Your mother cut her finger.
33 The wind blew the tree down.
34 The angry dog bit the boy's leg.
35 They stood in the rain for an hour.